God's Call: Why I Entered the Seminary

My Religious Vocation and Journey Vol. 1

Vivencio Ballano

Published by Vivencio Ballano, 2024.

While every precaution has been taken in the preparation of this book, the publisher assumes no responsibility for errors or omissions, or for damages resulting from the use of the information contained herein.

GOD'S CALL: WHY I ENTERED THE SEMINARY

First edition. October 25, 2024.

Copyright © 2024 Vivencio Ballano.

ISBN: 979-8227836434

Written by Vivencio Ballano.

Also by Vivencio Ballano

Gender and the Catholic Church
Why Can't Pope Francis and the Catholic Church Fully Accept the LGBTQI?: A Sociological-Synodal Exploration and Solution
"We are God's Children Too!": Resisting Homophobia and Natural Law for Full LGBTQI Integration in the Catholic Church
"We're Not an Ideology But Persons With Human Dignity"

My Religious Vocation and Journey Vol. 1
God's Call: Why I Entered the Seminary

Watch for more at https://www.researchgate.net/profile/Vivencio-Ballano/stats.

Table of Contents

God's Call: Why I Entered the Seminary (My Religious Vocation and Journey Vol. 1) 1
    Chapter I 2
    Chapter 2 20
    Chapter 3 33
    Chapter 4 44

To My Deceased Parents Rosendo Sr. and Felicidad, and Grandmother Petronila

God's Call:
Why I Entered the Seminary
My Religious Vocation and Journey Vol. 1

Credit: Wikimedia/Free-Images.com

Vivencio O. Ballano

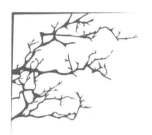

Chapter I

The Story of My of Calling

Photo: meditation_green_pray_forest.jpg   **Credit**: Pixabay/Free-Images.com

There are only very few professional sociologists who do research on the life of priests, sociological theology, sociological ethics and moral theology in the Roman Catholic Church. And as a Catholic, I feel God is

calling me to this type of scholarly work in the Church. Sociology, which specializes in the scientific study of social behavior and society is rarely appreciated in the Catholic Church.

One of the most popular sociologists in the Catholic Church, the late Fr. Andrew Greely, once observed the apathy of the Catholic bishops towards sociological research: Who needs it? He argued that,

> the Church...assumes that it has a monopoly on truth. Not only does it not make mistakes; it also knows everything that it needs to know about every possible subject. It understands whatever needs to be understood about human social behavior because of the revelations of God through Jesus to the Church and especially to the Pope. Thus, the Church can really learn nothing important from empirical research. At best, such research is a minor help; at worst, it is an obstacle to the Church's work" (Greely 1989, 393).

These assumptions are still popular among bishops and clerics who are educated in the normative disciplines of philosophy and theology in Catholic seminaries, colleges, and universities. In the general, the Catholic Church is afraid of the positivism and scientific research and debunking of modern sociology. This apathy can be traced to earlier centuries when the Catholic Church viewed the modern sciences as dangerous and heretical and Catholic philosophy as the only way of knowing the truth and upholding the Christian faith.

Because of the anti-modernist and anti-science ecclesial policies initiated by popes in late 19th and early 20th centuries, specifically the imposition of the Oath against Modernism on Catholic theologians and intellectuals by Pope Pius X, modern sciences such as sociology has been sidelined in the Catholic Church. Thomism, Scholastic philosophy, philosophical theology became the primary academic disciplines used by Catholic theologians, scholars, and ecclesiastics.

Throughout my ten years of seminary training, I studied philosophy and theology but not the scientific discipline of modern sociology. I can still remember my first sociology course in the college seminary called "Introduction to Sociology," taught not by a sociologist but a priest who was my seminary Rector and who only studied philosophy and theology! Our class only used one introduction to sociology textbook, which was used by my Rector as a guide for him to give philosophical reflections of the text! In short, I never learned sociology throughout my priestly training.

And yet modern sociology, which was founded by the Emile Durkheim, is a crucial and much-needed academic discipline for bishops, priests, and theologians as the Catholic Church is facing a vastly complex contemporary world whereby preaching the Gospel and achieving the church mission require scientific understanding of behavioral patterns and evolving social structures before applying church doctrines and dogmas. The Church needs to know people's behavior, human culture, and social structure if it aims to evangelize the world as mandated by Christ. It cannot just view society from afar and judge its morality using deductive analysis of philosophy without inductive sociological research.

For instance, the issue on LGBTQI inclusion in the Catholic Church requires sociological research to fully comprehend the gay community's gender experiences in society. It cannot be resolved by mere philosophical reasoning using the age-long natural law theory. I published two academic sociological books on LGBTQI inclusivity in the Church to clarify the difference between the Church's philosophical-theological view of sex and gender and the inductive sociological view.

The fear of several bishops and Catholic theologians that sociology is teaching secularism, positivism, and mechanistic view of society that tend to oppose church teachings is largely unfounded. Sociology as the scientific study of social behavior and society only aims to describe and understand behavioral and social patterns of modern and contemporary society. It is generally value-free in judgment using the scientific method. It does not aim to attack church doctrines and undermine the spiritual mission of the Catholic Church.

The devout Catholic sociologist Thomas Luckman (2023) has rightly argued that sociologists have no business debunking and delegitimating religion and religious beliefs such as the Catholic religion and its religious doctrines. Religion deals with the supernatural, while sociology, as a science, deals with the empirical and the natural world of the senses. Sociology cannot the scientific basis of religion since its beliefs is beyond empirical experience and scientific investigation.

Despite this difference, one cannot also deny that religion is social in nature since it is part of human culture and society. Religious thoughts and practices are also human acts. Thus, modern sociology has a crucial role to assist religion and theology to articulate the social aspects of religious beliefs. As a hindsight, I feel that sociological research needs to be incorporated in Catholic theology as the behavioral or empirical foundation of some of its moral and doctrinal teachings. Sociology, for instance, is highly important for the application and social analysis of the Catholic Church's set of social doctrines called Catholic social teaching, a set of moral principles that aim to apply the Christian faith in modern and contemporary societies.

Looking back, years after I left the seminary training, I realized that now that God is calling me to enter the seminary not to become a priest but to become a sociologist for priests and the Catholic Church. There is a strong urge within me that God is calling me to popularize modern sociology in the Church and establish a sort of sociological theology and sociological ethics in Catholic scholarship. This is indeed a daunting task. It requires great minds such as those of St. Augustine, St. Thomas Aquinas, Karl Rahner, or Hans Kung, to name a few!

Thus, in my prayers, I asked the God, "Why me, Lord?" There are many brilliant minds in the Catholic Church. Although I always belong to the top section out of several sections during my grade school and high school, I was not really the class valedictorian and the most academic person in my batch. I was educated in public school. I did not receive Catholic education before I enter the seminary. Like most of the seminarians who joined our local diocesan seminary during my time, I belong to the working class.

I was busy helping my poor parents in our small food business to survive. I was not the most academic and brilliant student in my high school batch. When I was passed the entrance examination of the top Jesuit university in Manila for my theological studies, after graduating from a college diocesan seminary in the province, there were several more brilliant students than me who graduated with Latin honors such as summa cum laude, magna laude, and cum laude, who came from middle-class families and who graduated from this top Catholic university.

I remember the story of my Rector in our college seminary that his classmate, Cardinal Antonio Tagle, the current pro-prefect of the Vatican's Dicastery for the Evangelization of Peoples, always got straight A's or excellent grades at the end of every semester at the Jesuit-run Ateneo de Manila University. Tagle graduated *Summa Cum Laude* in college. He was a brilliant student. He even finished his doctorate in systematic theology with top honors from the prestigious Catholic University of America in Washington, DC, in the United States.

Although God has called him to be a bishop and top cardinal-administrator in the Catholic Church, Cardinal Tagle could have been the right person to receive God's call to initiate reforms in Catholic scholarship and introduce sociological theology in the Catholic Church. That is why I kept asking the Lord, why me?

While I was studying theology at the Ateneo's Loyola School of Theology, I was also surrounded and taught by great and brilliant Jesuit mentors, scholars, and authors such as Fr. John N. Schumacher, SJ, Fr. Thomas H. Green, SJ, Fr. Joseph J. Smith, SJ, Fr. Romeo Intengan, SJ, Fr. Mario Francisco, SJ, and so forth. Why not they, Lord? These Jesuits eventually became my inspiration and role model to be a scholar and author for the Catholic Church!

When I joined the religious priesthood and entered the Jesuit Novitiate (preliminary formation for religious priesthood), my batchmates were brilliant graduates with honors from top and prestigious universities in the Philippines. As novices, we were all college graduates and professionals. One is a linguist, a teacher, a sociologist, and one is even a medical doctor who is now a Jesuit Missionary in Timor-Leste.

Why me? I did not receive any top honors when I finished my master's in theology five years after I left the Jesuit training and started teaching in a Catholic College in the City of Manila run by sisters in 1991. I guess my former professors and classmates at the Loyola School of Theology are probably surprised to see my posts and links of my peer-reviewed scholarly books and journal articles on modern sociology and Catholic theology in my seminary and theological school websites. Some probably remembered me only an artist and saxophonist but not as an intellectual or intelligent student while I was studying at the Ateneo.

God's call is indeed mysterious. If God indeed is calling me to be a Catholic sociologist and incorporate sociology in Catholic theology and Christian ethics, I would kneel with full humility before our Lord and ask Him to guide me and show me the way. I often pray to the Holy the Spirit for enlightenment before starting to write my book chapters or journal articles.

To enter the Catholic seminary to undergo priestly training not to become a priest but a Catholic sociologist who would be doing research about priests and the Catholic Church in contemporary times is beyond my comprehension. But I feel that God is calling towards this type of vocation. This book is the first part of personal story about my religious calling and journey in the Catholic Church as a believer and Catholic sociologist.

Photo: Emile Durkheim, the French Founder of Modern Sociology
Credit: Wikimedia/Free-Images.com

Initial Calling

As Jesus was walking beside the Sea of Galilee, He saw two brothers, Simon called Peter and his brother Andrew. They were casting a net into the sea, for they were fishermen. "Come, follow[1]

---

1. https://biblehub.com/greek/1205.htm

GOD'S CALL: WHY I ENTERED THE SEMINARY

Me," [2] Jesus said,[3] "and[4] I will make[5] you[6] fishers[7] of men." [8] And at once they left their nets and followed Him... (Matthew 4: 18-20)

After He ascended to heaven, Jesus calls His disciples through ordinary events and circumstances. He does not necessarily appear in person or in one's dream. He normally calls people through ordinary human experience.

I think the story of my vocation began when I was in senior high school. I am a product of the public school system where religious classes or catechism are not offered in school curriculum. So, I was surprised when one day a group of missionaries distributed small bibles in our classroom and taught us about God. After their talk, they gave us small white bibles of the King James version. Since the missionaries were Protestants and I was raised up by my parents as a Catholic, I did not bother to read my copy. However, I kept it safe in our house.

With the influence of my cousin Boboy who took up flying to become a pilot, I decided to go to Manila to follow his path. However, flying school is expensive. You need a lot of money to finish the required number of flying hours to get a license to become a commercial pilot. He himself was not able to finish his fling course. He shifted to an accounting course in college.

My cousin Boboy advised me to first take up an aeronautical engineering first before seriously pursuing a flying course to become a pilot. He said I could be a flight engineer since it the nearest way to be in

---

2. https://biblehub.com/greek/1473.htm

3. https://biblehub.com/greek/3004.htm

4. https://biblehub.com/greek/2532.htm

5. https://biblehub.com/greek/4160.htm

6. https://biblehub.com/greek/4771.htm

7. https://biblehub.com/greek/231.htm

8. https://biblehub.com/greek/444.htm

the same plane with a commercial pilot. Maybe one day, he said, I could finance my own flying hours to become a professional pilot.

Photo: Philippine Jeepney at UP Manila **Credit:** Pixabay/Free-Images.com

I agreed with my cousin. So, after graduation I decided travel to Manila in 1980 and stayed with him to take up aeronautical engineering at Feati University, the oldest university offering aeronautics in the Philippines. I was determined then to become an aeronautical engineer and become a pilot. But before boarding the ship for Manila, I accidentally remembered the small bible I received during my senior year. I was thinking that this was my only divine protection for my new journey in life. But I just placed it the side pocket of my travelling bag before I took the boat for Manila, the capital city of the Philippines.

This was my first time I left my city to travel alone. I was determined to study in Manila. It was agreed that my cousin and his friend would meet in the port once I arrived there. Manila is much bigger and heavily populated than my own city.

I stayed with my cousin in a rented room and shared with him the expenses for food and lease. The environment was not conducive for studying since our room was on the second floor of a busy wet market on the ground floor and was adjacent to a busy jeepney terminal. It was

GOD'S CALL: WHY I ENTERED THE SEMINARY

indeed noisy outside our room, crowded with people buying in the wet market, commuters in the terminal, and passersby in the main road.

Photo: From the distance is Feati University along the Pasig River in Manila where I studied Aeronautical Engineering
Credit: Wikimedia/Free-Images.com

Moving On

To lessen expenses and live in a quiet and clean environment, I decided to transfer to my uncle Lucio's house in Queen's Row Subdivision in Bacoor, Cavite, at the start of the second semester, where my step grandmother stayed during the second semester. Being in a remote area, the subdivision was quite with a lot of fresh air, although quite far from my university in Manila. It took around two hours of travel.

I was comfortable in my uncle's home. My only major worry and expense is my daily fare. Food and lodging were free in his home. My main duty in the house is to help my grandmother and their house maid in cooking, cleaning the house and premises, house repair, and errands and chores for my uncle's young family.

One sign for a person to feel that he or she is not on his or her real vocation in life is dissatisfaction. I was happy and comfortable in my uncle's home. If I persisted, I could have finished my course and become an engineer. However, there was a growing dissatisfaction with my course. I felt that it did not correspond to my interest and talent. Engineering was too technical for me. Mathematics was not also my favorite subject. I discovered also that my interest was more on the liberal arts and humanities.

If the course is not really meant for you and God is calling somewhere else, there is always a feeling of dissatisfaction with what you are currently been doing or studying. After a few months studying my aeronautics course, I noticed that that the courses I am taking did fit into my academic interests. For one, there were a lot of math and computations, typical of an engineering course. Thus, I was struggling with my engineering math subjects, barely passing them, although I belonged to the top section in high school and the top 10 percent of the graduating class.

However, there was one course that caught my attention—an introductory course on religion and Christian values. I thought it was weird for an engineering course to have a one-unit course on religion. Although we only met one hour per week, I was nevertheless attracted to the lessons taught by my professor. This personal curiosity about religion and spiritual life has led me to go to our university library and read books on Stoicism, Greek philosophy, and St. Augustine of Hippo's "City of God" and "Confessions." I was particularly attracted to Augustine's "Confessions," a vivid autobiography and description of Augustine's conversion to the Catholic faith.

Saints Augustine and Ignatius of Loyola

St. Augustine of Hippo Africa was a great sinner before his conversion to Catholicism. As a young man, he led an immoral life. He had a son outside marriage. The following unforeseen event had led to his conversion to the Christian faith:

Sometime in the year 386, Augustine and his friend Alypius were spending time in Milan. While outdoors, Augustine heard the voice of a child singing a song, the words of which were, "Pick it up and read it. Pick it up and read it." He thought at first that the song was related to some kind of children's game but could not remember ever having heard such a song before.

Then, realizing that this song might be a command from God to open and read the Scriptures, he located a Bible, picked it up, opened it and read the first passage he saw. It was from the Letter of Paul to the Romans. Augustine read:

Not in carousing and drunkenness, not in sexual excess and lust, not in quarreling and jealousy. Rather, put on the Lord Jesus Christ, and make no provision for the desires of the flesh.
—Romans 13: 13-14.

Reading this scripture, Augustine felt as if his heart were flooded with light. He turned totally from his life of sin. He was baptized by Ambrose during the Easter Vigil April 24, 387. His friend Alypius and his son Adeodatus were baptized at the same time. (Midwest Augustinians n.d., paras.4-7).

Augustine eventually became one of the great theologians and writers in the Catholic Church.
One line of his "Confessions" that greatly struck me and influenced me to seriously pursue the spiritual life was his famous passage: "You have made us for yourself, O Lord, and our heart is restless until it rests in you." Indeed, reading St. Augustine's life has made realized that there is another dimension of life beyond the material world—the spiritual life with God.

Another great saint who was converted to Christ by reading the Bible and became the founder of the largest religious order of Catholic priests and brothers in the Roman Catholic Church is St. Ignatius of Loyola, a Basque Spaniard soldier before his personal conversion. Like Augustine, Ignatius was also a great sinner before becoming a soldier for Christ!

While being bored recuperating from his fatal wound in the Castle of Loyola after his leg was hit by a cannonball in the Battle of Pamplona, Spain in 1521, Ignatius asked for favorite: romances of chivalry. But lo! The only books available in the castle were the Bible and Lives of the Saints. Without a choice, Ignatius started reading these books and experienced a spiritual conversion and strong desire to do great things for Christ! While reading, he asked himself: If the saints can do this for Christ, why shouldn't I? Thus, his dreams of achieving heroic feats on the battlefield became burning desires to serve Christ and His Church!

Photo: St. Ignatius of Loyola **Credit**: Wikimedia/Free-Images.com

Like St. Augustine and St. Ignatius of Loyola, I also started my spiritual journey by reading the Bible. Although my family is Catholic and my mother is a deeply religious woman, I was not a devout Catholic who regularly attend Sunday masses and received catechism in our parish. Like most Catholics in the country who are baptized and are not active in church rituals and activities in their parishes, we belong to what the Catholic Church calls as 'the unchurched", that is, baptized Catholic who are religious but not active in our parish church. In sociology of religion, this type of people care called "spiritual but not religious."

I am no saint and my own conversion pales in comparison with that of St. Augustine and St. Ignatius. But I noticed some similarities. I was indeed converted to Christ by accidentally reading the Bible for the first time. I could not even remotely compare myself with the life of St. Augustine and St. Ignatius and their conversion stories. But one thing is certain for me—that like Augustine and Ignatius, my spiritual journey and religious calling in life with Christ started with encountering Christ through his words in the gospels.

I recalled that the following Christ's words in the gospel had struck my innermost being and opened my eyes to the importance of spiritual life—that life is more than the material things and human attachments we enjoy on this earth! Christ said:

> For whosoever will save his life shall lose it; but whosoever shall lose his life for my sake and the gospel's, the same shall save it.
>
> For what shall it profit a man, if he shall gain the whole world, and lose his own soul?
>
> Or what shall a man give in exchange for his soul? (King James Version, Mark 8: 35-37)

After reading and reflecting His words, I started to become disinterested with what I am pursuing in my life. I began to question my course and ambition to become a pilot and aeronautical engineer. What for? I asked myself, If I become a successful commercial pilot and see the world, what is next? Would this make a true disciple of Christ? I may gain the whole world but will lose my own soul in the process. Jesus is emphatic in the gospel: I am the way, the truth, and the life! No one goes to God the Father except through me!

The stories of Jesus in the gospels had made me a changed man. Thanks to the lay missionaries who gave me a copy of the Bible during high school. It became my spiritual guide to discover Christ for my life. During my spare time, I read the Bible and followed Christ's journey. While reading the gospels, I began imaginatively entering the scenes of the gospel that I was reading. I felt I was personally in front of Jesus listening to His words.

After I entered the seminary, I realized that this type of prayer technique is called contemplation. I was blessed in my life to have the famous spiritual writer and author Fr. Thomas "Tom" Green, SJ., as my spiritual director while at the theological seminary. He is a best-selling author of spirituality books. He was also a great friend. He was also one of my Jesuit mentors who inspired to become an author and a scholar.

Fr. Tom taught on how to contemplate the scenes of the gospel I was reading as a prayer technique. Contemplation is different from meditation since the former utilizes more the person's imagination in entering the story of the Scriptures while latter involves pondering or reflecting the message of the biblical text to one's life. The Bible Gateway Website describe the distinction between contemplation and meditation using the Bible passages.

> **Contemplation:** This is one of the most essential aspects for building a growing relationship with the Lord...[pray-ers] have a feeling of closeness and intimacy with the Lord. One of the most valuable things that you can do with this feeling is to relax and embrace it. Just *be* with God. You don't need to always be talking at God. In this stage, simply sit in the presence of God and feel his tender love and embrace.

GOD'S CALL: WHY I ENTERED THE SEMINARY 17

Meditation: Think about what the parts [of the Bible passages] that stood out to you meant to the original audience and what the author might have been thinking when he wrote it. Think about the specific part of the passage that spoke directly to you. Focus intently on why the Holy Spirit might have chosen these words to speak to you. Reflect on how it might connect to your life. Is it relevant to something that you are going through? Do certain people come to mind whom God may want you to reach out to or reconcile with?[1]

Photo: Meditation_calm_above_city.jpeg Credit: Pixabay/Free-Images.com

Reading the small bible which was given to me during my fourth-year high school and was kept in my bag was accidental. I only opened and read it after more than five months studying in Manila. I could still remember that I first open and read this bible in one morning while being bored inside my room after doing my chores of cooking and cleaning my uncle's house.

The irony is that longer I stayed in the seminary formation, I more I lost the sense of wonder and contemplation in reading the Gospels.

Because of the dominance of philosophy, theology, and reasoning in my clerical education, where almost every story in the Bible and elements of the Christian faith was given a hermeneutic, historical, and scientific explanation, I felt I gradually lost the sense of contemplation in prayer and the "feeling" of being a new convert in the Christian faith I initially encountered when I first read the Bible.

I just can't personally imagine why I entered the Catholic seminary to become a priest but ended up becoming a professional sociologist for priests, studying their life and difficulties closely through sociological lens! People are indeed historical and open system. They actualize their being gradually in society through their response to social and historical events. We can't be sure how we can shape your life as go through history. There are a lot of things in our life that we cannot anticipate. These are the unforeseen events that can determine our life as we grow up. Thus, no matter how we control our life to attain our plans, there are always unforeseen or unanticipated events that can alter the course of our life.

God generally reveals His call through ordinary human experiences and events. At first, the call may be vague to person received it. But He will gradually clarify His call and reveal His will in subsequent events and human experiences. In my case, Christ did not reveal Himself to me personally nor He appeared in my dream. He revealed Himself through His words in the gospel I was reading. He never directly told me to enter the seminary to become a priest in order to serve Him! In fact, this was my interpretation after meditating His words. However, future historical events in my life and personal experiences inside the seminary had slowly revealed His will for me. Christ called me to follow Him but not as a priest but something else beyond the priesthood!

References

Greely, Andrew. 1989. "Sociology and the Catholic Church: Four Decades of Bitter Memories." *Sociological Analysis 50(4) Fiftieth Anniversary Special Issue* (Winter, 1989): 393-397.

Midwest Augustinians. n.d. "Conversion of St. Augustine." Available at: https://www.midwestaugustinians.org/conversion-of-st-augustine

Chapter 2

God Calls Through Human Events and Circumstances

P hoto: Christ, the Redeemer **Credit**: Pixabay/Free-Images.com

God really speaks through human events and people. It is rare that He interferes with natural events and people's affairs unless necessary to pursue His plan. This is the mystery of the Incarnation when God became human. God became one of us except sin to make Himself present and felt in human events and affairs.

The incarnation symbolizes the metaphysical and empirical aspect of the Christian faith and preaching. In incarnation, the Word became flesh and dwelt among us (John 1: 1–18). This symbolizes the reality that the supernatural truth about God is enmeshed with the empirical reality of the world once this truth became flesh and preached in human culture. (Ballano 2019, 7)

As the Ministry Magazine (2007) aptly explains:

When God spoke to people in Bible times, such as when He appeared to Moses at the burning bush (Exod. 3[1]), there was little room for doubt that it was God. However, God didn't always speak in such a spectacular fashion—such as when He, on one occasion, spoke to Elijah in a gentle whisper (1 Kings 19:11[2], 12[3]).

We often listen for the grandiose voice of God—and sometimes God speaks that way. More often, however, the voice of God comes through more subtly than that. Often God speaks through our quiet moments, through other people, and through life's circumstances. In a crowded world of noise and life's distractions, sometimes we have a hard time understanding what God says.

"Christ did not come to condemn the world but to embrace and bless it along with its culture. Christ above culture underscores an approach which is synthetic. Christ is the Lord who is both of this world and of the other" (Omollo 2016, 114). Since God has saved the world thorough His Son, human experience has been sanctified and divine will

---

1. https://ref.ly/Exod.%203;esv?t=biblia

2. https://ref.ly/1%20Kings%2019.11;esv?t=biblia

3. https://ref.ly/1%20Kings%2019.12;esv?t=biblia

can be expressed in human culture, although the religious mission to Christianize is always there to be fulfilled by believers.

Through the mystery of the Incarnation, the human and the divine have been merged just as Christ become both man and divine. People can now discover God's presence through human experiences and historical events sanctified by Christ through His death and resurrection. God's call can be discovered though prayer and discernment. Discovering God's will not always be miraculous. People always expect some supernatural signs to know His will.

However, in most cases, God speaks through genuine human experience and external events. He normally manifests His will through human experience and divine creation. God specifically reveals Himself through the Bible. An encounter with Christ by reading the Gospel is a direct way of encountering God. That's why great saints in the Catholic Church were all converted to Christ by personally encountering Him through the Bible. Reading the Bible and encountering Christ in the gospels are direct means to know and feel God's presence in our lives

In my own little way, my accidental reading of the Bible way back in 1981 was my starting point of my religious vocation and spiritual journey. But again, this event would not have happened without a series of events that God has silently prepared for me such as lay missionaries who distributed small bibles in our classroom when I was in fourth year high school in 1980. I could not have read my own copy if did not transfer to my uncle's place, which provided me with the serene and quiet environment conducive to reflection and prayer.

My previous rented place was in the middle of a busy street and on top of a wet market. I could not have been forced to read my bible if there were other books and magazines available in my uncle's house. I already finished my chores on that morning and was looking for something to read. None was available in the room except the bible placed inside the side pocket of my bag before I left for Manila.

I find this accidental reading of the Bible to be similar to the experience of St. Ignatius of Loyola, the founder of the Jesuit Order, which I later entered after seven years of diocesan seminary formation. While bored recuperating from his fatal wound in the Castle of Loyola after his leg was hit by a cannonball, Ignatius asked for books he loved reading: romances of chivalry. But was forced to ready only the books available in the place—the Bible and a Lives of the Saints. Ignatius was converted as a soldier of Christ after reading the Bible and became the founder of the largest and most powerful religious order of priests and brothers in the Catholic Church—the Society of Jesus or popularly known as the Jesuits. The Jesuits played a crucial role during the counter-reformation to check the advance of Protestantism in Europe and reenkindled the Christian faith during the 16th century.

I had not prior knowledge about the religious order founded by St. Ignatius since I did not attend any of the Jesuit schools and universities in the Philippines. However, I now realized some similarity between my conversion and St. Ignatius's. We were both inspired by Christ's life in the Bible to serve the Church, although I am no great saint like St. Ignatius. This similarity of finding Christ through reading of the Bible was one reason why I was attracted to the Jesuits and later joined the religious order as a scholastic or seminarian.

The Inspiration of Pope John Paul II

Photo: Pope John Paul II Credit: Wikimedia/Free-Images.com

After continuously reading my bible for two weeks, I became interested in attending the Holy Mass, the summit of Christian life for Catholics. I started to visit and attend regularly the Holy Mass and religious activities of our subdivision's chapel. A priest normally visits this chapel for Sunday and Wednesday Masses as well as First Friday Mass and fiesta celebration. Our subdivision chapel had become a mini parish. The parishioners were increasing in number. Masses were often full. Lay ministers, lectors, altar servers, and chapel organizations were active during Eucharistic celebrations.

Aside from reading the Bible and life of Christ in the gospels, one important person who inspired me to become a priest was St. Pope John Paul II when visited Manila in January 1990. It was also the time I started discovering Christ life in the Bible while residing in my uncle's house. For me, Pope John Paul II, who is now a canonized saint in the Catholic Church, was my inspiration why I decided to enter the seminary. During his first visit in Manila in 1981, I intently listened to his inspiring sermons and followed his activities on the television.

Unsatisfied of seeing him on TV, waited patiently his convoy and papal car in one of the streets of Manila to see him personally. I saw the pope waving at us as he passed by the overcrowded street. The

Philippines is the third largest Catholic country in the world, next only to Mexico and Brazil. In international religiosity surveys, the Filipinos are consistently among most religious people in the world. On his second visit to the Philippines last January 15, 1995, Saint Pope John Paul II broke attendance record where approximately four million Filipinos attended his holy mass celebrated at the Quirino Grandstand and Luneta Park in Manila to celebrate World Youth Day—a sign that indeed Filipinos are very religious people in the world.

For me, seeing the pope in person even only in a very short moment was like seeing Christ in person! Pope John Paul II exuded holiness, peace, and charism. I did sense during this moment his strong faith and sanctity. This personal encounter with him and his inspiring homilies and speeches during his visit in the Philippines in February 1981 had greatly persuaded me to become a priest and imitate his holy life. I never told anyone about this personal transformation and spiritual influence caused by the pope's visit in Manila. Like the Blessed Virgin Mary in the gospel, I kept this all in my heart.

My Burning Bush!

Reading and meditating Christ's life in the Bible passages and Pope John Paul's inspiration all played a crucial influence in my personal encounter with God—my burning bush, just as Moses personally encountered God in Horeb:

> Now Moses was tending the flock of Jethro his father-in-law, the priest of Midian, and he led the flock to the far side of the wilderness and came to Horeb, the mountain of God. There the angel of the Lord appeared to him in flames of fire from within a bush. Moses saw that though the bush was on fire it did not burn up. So Moses thought, "I will go over and see this strange sight—why the bush does not burn up." When the Lord saw that he had gone over to look, God called to him from within the bush, "Moses! Moses!"

And Moses said, "Here I am." (NIV Exodus 3:1-4)

Moses calling was dramatic and miraculous. God appeared to him a burning bush. But God's may not always be miraculous. He often speaks through human events and experience. Some people who entered the religious life are inspired by people they encountered. Some people decided to become a priest because of their childhood experience as altar boys. The parish priest inspired them to enter the seminary and become priest. Others got their vocation by reading the bible and lives of the saints such as the life St. Augustine and St. Ignatius.

I can still remember the most significantly day of my life when I decided to devote my life serving Christ. It was during the Ash Wednesday celebration, the beginning of Lent, the celebration of Christ's passion and death. I remember I fasted during this day and visited the chapel early, an hour earlier before the start of the Holy Mass and giving of ash. The putting of the ash symbolizes our frailty, God created us from dust and in dust we shall return!

The chapel opened early probably 4:30 o'clock in the afternoon and Ash Wednesday Mass started at 6:00 o' clock in the evening. I knelt before the altar and Blessed Sacrament and prayed fervently to God and so sorry for my sins more than an hour. I asked for God's guidance and sign where and how He was calling me to serve Him in the Church. This was fervently meditating this passage of Christ's temptation while kneeling, reminding that man does live by bread alone, that fleeting wealth, power, and fame of this world is nothing compared to God (Matthew 4: 1-11):

> The spirit led Jesus into the desert to be tempted by the Devil. After forty days and nights without food, Jesus was hungry. The Devil tempted Jesus to turn stones into bread, to which he replied, "Human beings cannot live on bread alone, but need every word God speaks." The second temptation was for Jesus to throw himself from the highest point of the temple

GOD'S CALL: WHY I ENTERED THE SEMINARY

and order angels to catch him. Jesus replied, "Do not put the Lord your God to the test." Finally, the Devil offered Jesus all the kingdoms of the world in return for worshipping him. Jesus replied, "Worship the Lord your God and serve only him!" The Devil left Jesus, and angels came and helped him.

I was thinking at the time that God has called me to serve our chapel by volunteering in cleaning the church premises. And indeed, I volunteered to clean and sweep the chapel after the Ash Wednesday. However, deep within me I felt that our Lord Jesus is calling me beyond volunteer work in the chapel. But how? When I was in fourth year high school, I remembered that a certain Redemptorist brother invited us to a lunch and vocation orientation on the priesthood and religious life in the Parish of the Holy Redeemer in my home city. It was a whole day affair. All of us classmates who participated actively during the orientation. However, when the religious brother who invited us asked the group of who us were interested to enter the seminary and become priests, all of us became silent. No one wanted to live a life of celibacy for priests!

This prior experience has given me an idea where God was probably leading me in His call. If the Lord is calling me for greater things, not just volunteering to clean our village chapel and do chores for the parish, becoming a priest entered my mind as my religious vocation and calling. My previous encounter with the Redemptorist brother during our vocation orientation for the priesthood in high school had guided me in my next step to discover God's call for my life. I knew what to do: Go home to my city and apply for the college seminary.

During high school, the religious redemptorist brother who attempted to recruit us to the priesthood gave us male students of the tope section a series of entrance examination to determine who among us were academically qualified to enter the seminary. One of my classmates named Danny who became our class salutatorian top the entrance examinations. He was my best friend in high school. He told me that after he topped the entrance examination, the religious brother "courted" the school and his parents to influence him to enter the seminary. Apparently, Danny had no vocation to the priesthood. He said he just one to test himself if he can whether he was ready to pass college scholarships in our last year in high school. He belonged to a poor family. His only way to get a college degree is to the pass entrance examinations of various scholarships.

Danny felt that he was a bit pressured by the religious brother and his religious congregation to enter the seminary. Luckily, he said, the result of his entrance examination the Philippine Military Academy (PMA), the premier military school in the country, was released before the graduation. And a telegram informed him that he was among the top passers of the exam and that should report to military school after the graduation. He felt relieved of the pressure from the religious brother to enter the seminary. Me and other classmates passed the entrance examination administered by the religious brother. But none of us entered the seminary.

Recalling this event, I now realized why none of us who took the entrance examination and wanted to become priest—we're all heterosexual and we don't want to profess the religious vow of a lifetime celibacy. We realized that by becoming priests we could no longer marry and raise our own family.

Scared of Celibacy?

The primary reason why I refused to enter the seminary after a religious brother gave us a vocation seminary during my fourth year in high school is celibacy. To become a Catholic priest implies living a life of perpetual celibacy and chastity. An ordained priest under Canon law or the law of the Catholic Church once ordained profess the vow of celibacy. He can no longer enter a valid sacramental marriage in the Church. If the priest leaves the ministry without dispensation from the Pope for his vow to celibacy and marries a woman in a civil wedding,

GOD'S CALL: WHY I ENTERED THE SEMINARY 29

he can automatic excommunication or expulsion from the Church according to Canon Law.

In the Catholic Church, those who enter the priesthood, religious or diocesan, are required to take the vow of celibacy. 'Celibacy' comes from the Latin word *coelebs*, which means an unmarried man. "Celibacy is a publicly committed state of living chastely, whereby the person, accepting the gift of God and identifying with Jesus Christ, freely chooses not to marry for the sake of the kingdom of God while serving God and other people" (Daly 2009, 21). It is a religious vow to "live a celibate, chaste life that is prohibitive of marriage and sexual behavior in order to facilitate priests' full devotion of service to the Church" (Issaco, Sahker, and Krinock 2015).

Christ's words in the gospel had given me the strength to overcome this fear of celibacy when I entered St. Peter Seminary in 1981. I was already resigned to the fact that I would be celibate throughout my life if ordained after my seminary formation, which would last ten years or more. I was so convinced that God called me to become a priest that I did not consider my limited experience with women before I enter the seminary. I did not foresee during my early years in seminary formation that mandatory celibacy would eventually be my major issue as I progressed in priestly training.

The Catholic Church assumes that once a candidate enters the priestly formation and faithfully obeys the seminary rules on chastity and fulfills the academic and spiritual requirements, he would receive the gift or charism of celibacy once ordained to the priesthood. It forgets that personal maturity in personality and sexuality is realistically acquired through normal socialization with the opposite sex in society and not in an isolated and all-male exclusive community of the seminary.

Seminarians will indeed grow in their academic, spiritual, and pastoral life but not in psychosexual life. No amount of personality and sexuality seminars in the seminary can substitute actual human experience in society. I published an entire research book or monograph entitled "Celibacy, Seminary Formation, and Catholic Clerical Sexual Abuse" to highlight the negative unintended of isolating seminarians in priestly formation and suppressing married priesthood that could lead to clerical sexual abuse, a persistent moral problem hounding the Catholic Church for decades.

Conversely, celibacy is not always a requirement to become a priest in the Catholic Church. In fact, St. Peter and most of Christ's apostles and disciples were married men. Christ taught in the gospels that celibacy is a rare gift. It is only given to a few and not to everyone. Thus, He did not require his disciples to become celibates as a requirement to follow him, although He himself is celibate.

A closer look at the RCC's history reveals that obligatory celibacy was not always an essential requirement for the priesthood. As a matter of fact, the Church today acknowledges that no law of celibacy as we know it today existed in the beginning (Kasomo 2012). Sipe (1990) argued that celibacy was freely decided by early church leaders themselves and was not imposed in the apostolic church. Some apostles, including Peter, were married, and never left their families during their ministry (Crosby 2003).

St. Paul also did not impose celibacy to his followers in view of the coming of the end times. The early ordained priests in the RCC were also married and only professed perpetual chastity after they became widowed (Brown 2008). Finally, some Church Fathers were also married while in ministry (Mayblin 2018).

It took the RCC a thousand years to impose mandatory celibacy. Jesus himself only recommended optional celibacy (Matthew 19:3–12). During the early years of Christianity, celibacy was only a voluntary ascetic practice of early Christian monks and some clerics, but not a universal practice for Catholic priests. Sipe (1990) cited a shred of interesting evidence showing the persistence married priesthood during the early Church and even identified some popes who were sons of popes and nine who were sons of either bishops or priests.

Historically, "official recommendations that priests should avoid marriage started to appear in the 5th century, but they were more or less ignored until the 12th century when the clamping down on priestly marriage, and the purging of women and priestly offspring from the Church took off with a vengeance" (Mayblin 2018, 5). Mandatory celibacy only became a universal norm after the Second Lateran Council in 1339, which was affirmed by the Council of Trent in 1563 and preserved up to the present (Owen 2001).

References

Ballano, Vivencio O. 2020. "Inculturation, Anthropology, and the Empirical Dimension of Evangelization." *Religions* 11(101): 1-14.

Crosby, Michael H. 2003. *Rethinking Celibacy, Reclaiming the Church*. Eugene, Oregon: Wipf and Stock.

Daly, Brendan. 2009. "Priestly Celibacy: The Obligations of Continence and Celibacy for Priests." *Compass: A Review of Topical Theology* 43(4): 20-34.

Issaco, Anthony, Ethan Sahker, and Elizabeth Krinock. 2015. "How Religious Beliefs and Practices Influence the Psychological Health of Catholic Priests." *American Journal of Men's Health* 10 (4): 325-337.

Kasomo, Daniel. 2012. "The Psychology Behind Celibacy." *International Journal of Psychology and Behavioral Sciences* 2 (4): 88-93. https://doi.org/10.5923/j.ijpbs.20120204.03.

Mayblin, Maya. 2019. "A Brilliant Jewel: Sex, Celibacy, and the Roman Catholic Church." Religion 49(4): 517-538.

Ministry Magazine. April 2007. 'God's Voice Through Our Circumstances[4].' https://www.ministrymagazine.org/archive/2007/04/gods-voice-through-our-circumstances.html

Omollo, Fredrick Otieno. 2016. Theoretical Discussions of Inculturation for Transformative Evangelization: Approaches from Intellectual History of African Catholic Theological Heritage and Voices from the Grassroots. *Human Dignity Journal* 63: 111–22.

---

4. https://www.ministrymagazine.org/

Owen, Helen. 2001. "When Did the Catholic Church Decide Priests Should Be Celibate?" *History News Network*. Available at https://historynewsnetwork.org/article/696

Sipe, A.W. Richard. 1990. *A Secret World: Sexuality and The Search for Celibacy 1st Edition*. East Sussex, UK: Brunner-Routledge.

Chapter 3

Entering the Seminary

Photo: Florence_seminary.jpeg **Credit:** Wikimedia/Free-Images.com

Towards the end of the second semester of my aeronautical course and after intense personal prayer, it dawned on me that God had probably been calling me to become a priest. St. Augustine's words were still fresh in my mind, "You have made us for yourself, O Lord, and our heart is restless until it rests in you." And Christ's words: "For what shall it profit a man, if he shall gain the whole world and lose his own soul? (Mark 8:36). With these words, I lost interest to become a commercial pilot and see the world! What for? I asked myself. I will enjoy all the comforts of life, but in the process will forget our Lord Jesus Christ, the source of life.

Right after the end of the second semester, I said goodbye to my grandmother and to Uncle Lucio and his family. Although I only stayed with the family for a few months, I already felt that I was part of the family. Thus, it was difficult for me to leave the place which I considered my second home. I would also miss the subdivision chapel, the sacred place where I encountered my burning bush and symbol of religious vocation.

Since I was hardworking during my stay and received no complaint against me, they persuaded me to stay and continue my course. But I was determined to follow where God was leading me. And there was only one place in my mind that I should need to do: Go back to my home city and enter the local diocesan seminary to become a priest!

My Parents' Initial Resistance

In the Philippines, having a priest in the family is prestige and a source of great pride for parents. Physicians, lawyers, and priests are among the most prestigious professions in the country. Thus, having a son as a priest is a sign of God's blessing for the family. There are even cases that the mothers would pressure their sons to become priests. So, it the mothers who have the real vocation to the priesthood not their sons.

I knew one priest who was forced to ordained because his mother has a strong vocation to the priesthood. Thus, after spending a few months as priest, he told his mother after that now that her wish had been granted after ordination, it was now his will that needed to be followed. Thus, he left the priesthood and soon became a family man.

My case seems different. When I broke the news that I would discontinue my engineering course and enter the seminary to become priest, my parents objected. They discouraged me to join the seminary since I would be earning income. It is often the custom among poor families that when the parents financed an elder child to finish college, he or she is expected to also help finance his or her younger sibling.

My parents supported my studies in Manila with the hope that when I finished my course, I would be responsible for the college education of my younger sisters.

Entering the priesthood would also mean that they cannot have grandchildren with me. In current Catholic priesthood, there is no option for married priesthood, although since the time of Christ, priests can be either celibate or married. It was only during the 12th and 13th centuries that married priesthood was suppressed by the Catholic Church, leaving celibate priesthood as the only option to be ordained as clerics.

After some convincing and prayer, my parents finally consented that I would be entering the college seminary for the new school year. Joining the seminary training would mean blessing in disguise. Parents would be free from their obligation to finance their sons' college education. During my time, the bishop and the diocese shouldered all the expenses for our food, board and lodging, and education. My parents would just give us some pocket money and weekly fare for our Sunday break.

Applying for the Seminary

Photo: writing_pen_man_boy.jpg Credit: Pixabay/Free-Images.com

Upon my arrival from Manila, I started to inquire how to enter St. Peter College Seminary, the only local seminary in our city. As a young man, I often saw this diocesan seminary, which is located a few kilometers away from the city. Although secluded, this seminary can be seen from the highway whenever we passed by the area. As a young man, I sometimes chanced to see some seminaries at the seminary gate wearing their white cassocks or white polo uniform and black pants whenever I passed by riding a jeepney.

I went to my parish, the St. Joseph Cathedral parish, and to inquired about the seminary entrance requirements. I really did not have any personal acquaintance with priests in our diocese before I entered the seminary. Although I am greatly influenced by mother's strong religiosity and devotion to the Virgin Mary by reciting the rosary at home, I was not a regular churchgoer in our parish. Like most Catholics in the country who are personally spiritual but not religious or churchgoers, I seldom attend Sunday masses and participate in parish activities in my church, but I belong to this parish.

That is why it immediately dawned on me to visit the Cathedral parish office and inquired about how to enter the local seminary. The parish secretary introduced me to Fr. Ely who was the Vocation Director of the diocese at that time, responsible for recruiting and screening applicants to the college seminary. Fr. Ely interviewed me right then and there in a room and asked mainly why I wanted to enter the seminary and become a priest. He inquired about my academic credentials. He was quite impressed upon knowing that I was a consistent honor student during my grad school and belonged to the top section throughout my high school years. It was rare to have applicants from top public and private school in the city who will apply for the seminary.

After the personal interview, Fr. Ely immediately informed that I passed the initial screening. He then scheduled my written entrance exam the following day. After two weeks, I learned that I passed this examination. Fr. Ely then visited our home and informed my parents that I will be entering St. Peter Seminary by June, the opening of classes for the new school year.

St. Peter Seminary was originally built as a high school seminary for boys of elite families in the 1970s but was transformed in the 1980s into a sub-regional college seminary for the formation of diocesan priests for the three dioceses of Tandag, Surigao, and Butuan. Conversely, the Catholic Church invented the seminary in the 16th century to improve the priestly training of diocesan priests.

Photo: st_francis_seminary_entrance.jpg Credit: Wikimedia/Free-Images.com

The Seminary as a Total Institution

One of the main reasons why me and my high school classmates declined to enter the seminary during our search in or vocation orientation before graduation is the isolation of the seminary from the rest of the world. No women and worldly pleasure inside the seminary. It is also located away from the city. Council of Trent's intention of establishing the seminary was to improve the academic, spiritual, and pastoral training of future diocesan priests away from the temptations of the city.

Before the Council of Trent established the seminary as the only institution for clerical training, candidates were given the flexibility of choosing a celibate or married priesthood in an apprenticeship style of clerical training. But with seminary clerical training, priests and seminarians are forced to disregard any possibility of pursuing married priesthood. Under the current seminary formation, it is assumed that seminarians can receive the gift of celibacy if they are open to the Holy Spirit and subservient to the seminary rules and practices.

The celibate seminary formation is founded on the obligatory clerical celibacy imposed by the Catholic Church in the Second and Fourth Lateran Councils. With this imposition, the Council of Trent later adopted the all-male and celibate seminary training in every diocese or group of dioceses for the training of secular priests in 16th century.

The sociologist Erving Goffman coined the term 'total institution" as "a place of residence and work where many situated individuals, cut off from the wider society for an appreciable length of time, together lead an enclosed, formally administered round of life (Goffman 1961, xiii). People who enter this type of organization are generally "cut off from the rest of society and are under almost total control of agents of the institution" (Henslin 2014, 3). Thus, institutionalized practices of total institutions are constructed not only to strip members of their former identity, but also of their humanity.

Dehumanization is often associated with total institutions as members undergo a constant surveillance of their behavior by authorities and forced to perform practices to achieve the institutional goals regardless of their negative consequences to the members humanity (Malacrida 2005). It causes significant problems for those who suffer from it. Dehumanization in total institutions promote anxiety or depression and reduces the need for competition and interaction, damaging their well-being (Ariño-Mateo et al. 2022).

A total institution that is isolated from the real world does not also offer a natural environment for authentic human growth. With the strong behavioral control of the institution's authorities, members are being forced to undergo human resocialization process that is often contrary to their personal and gender preferences (Scott 2011). A total institution is characterized by a bureaucratic control of the human needs of its members, functioning through a mortification of the self (Goodman 2013). A study by Valeries Jenness and Julie Gerlinger (2020) among transgender women in an American prison, for instance, revealed total institutions' dehumanizing environment and human suffering in a U.S. prison where transgender prisoners are forced to undergo resocialization to become male prisoners instead of allowing their transgender identity and personality to flourish.

In Goffman's description, total institutions have always functioned in accordance with its established internal rules that organize directly or indirectly the sex life of its members in which sexual relations are often limited, banned, and even sanctioned (Giami 2020). In this case, members have no choice to freely actualize their own human and sexual development in normal and real-life circumstances. The institution's set of rules determine what members ought to be as human beings.

The Seminary as a Total Institution

Photo: Author with his batchmates in the college seminary **Credit:** Author

Although not all aspects of Goffman's total institution are applicable to the spiritual and academic goals of Catholic seminary, its four elements such as "members living in the same place and under the same authority, batch living, rigid timetabling and scheduling of activities and an institutional goal of resocialization" (Scott 2010, 215) are evident in this type of organization. As a total institution, the seminary is "a place comprising residence, work, study, background, sociability and entertainment, where lots of people living alike but apart from the well-off society lead a reclusive life and formally administrated" (Benelli and DaCosta-Rosa 2002). Its members are governed by a set of ecclesial rules on clerical formation which is implemented by seminary formators led by the rector.

Despite the experiments of making seminary formation adapted to the current world by the Second Vatican Council (Vatican II), Catholic seminaries are generally total institution in structure institutionalized during the 16th century to replace apprenticeship as the primary method of clerical training since the time of Christ. Vatican II and post-conciliar documents on seminary formation still insisted on communal character of clerical formation, resembling to Goffman's specific description of TI.

The seminary college, for instance, was conceived of as "a self-sufficient place where those being prepared for priestly ordination, and those responsible for their education, lived and worked" (Oakley 2017, 223).

Like Goffman's total institutions, Catholic seminaries for priestly formation are generally done in the same place under the authority of the rector and seminary formators appointed by the bishop. All seminarians are treated alike and are required to follow the daily routine of praying, working, and studying. Despite slight cultural variations, all seminaries follow a regimented way of life determined and imposed by seminary formators. Lastly, the enforced activities are based on a rational plan of the Church's documents on seminary formation (e.g., *Optatam Totius* [Decree on Priestly Training] 1965; *Pastores Dabo Vobis* [On Formation of Priests in the Circumstances of the Present Day] 1992; *Ratio Fundamentalis Institutiones Sacerdotalis* [The Gift of the Priestly Vocation] 2016) to attain the official purpose of forming celibate priests as another Christ (*Alter Christus*), ready to administer the sacraments and manage the parishes for the faithful.

The Catholic Church teaches that "the heart of the spiritual formation in the seminary is rooted in the discipleship of Jesus experienced in the life of the one who offers himself for ordination as a priest. This is central to the future priest's identity and mission" (Oakley 2017, 230). Obedience to the will of God as expressed by ecclesiastical superiors, in the manner of Christ's obedience to God, as the way of becoming another Christ is the rational plan of the Catholic seminary formation. This plan attempts to create a new self-understanding and identity among seminarians as future celibate priests. The seminary had a set of operational rules, approved by the bishops, and administered by seminary rector, to be strictly obeyed by seminarians (Madden 2010).

"If celibacy becomes obligatory, then priests who have no gift to celibacy would obviously suffer the consequences of living a lonely celibate and asexual life in which they are not called for" (Ballano 2023, 2). It is silent martyrdom for candidates with vocation to married priesthood but must undergo a celibate seminary formation and live a life-long celibate lifestyle contrary to their social calling. Thus, Donald Cozzens (2006) rightly views obligatory clerical celibacy as

> a contradiction in terms, because celibacy is a charism, a gift, a grace that resides in the individual often before the person knows it in his heart ... If charismatic celibacy is indeed a jewel in the crown of the priesthood, mandated, obligatory celibacy for individuals not blessed with the charism is a silent martyrdom.

References

Ariño-Mateo, Eva, Ramírez-Vielma, Raúl, Arriagada-Venegas, Matías, Nazar-Carter, Gabriela, and Pérez-Jorge, David. 2022. "Validation of the Organizational Dehumanization Scale in Spanish-Speaking Contexts." *International Journal of Environment Research and Public Health,* 19(8), 4805; https://doi.org/10.3390/ijerph19084805.

Ballano, Vivencio O. 2023. *In Defense of Married Priesthood: A Sociotheological Investigation of Catholic Clerical Celibacy.* London: Routledge.

Benelli, Silvio José, and Da Costa-Rosa, Abilio. 2003. "Study About the Presbyterate Formation in a Catholic Seminary." *Psychology Studies (Campinas)[1]* 20 (3): https://doi.org/10.1590/S0103-166X2003000300008.

Cozzens, Donald. 2006. *Freeing Celibacy.* Collegeville, Minnesota: Liturgical Press.

Giami, Alain. 2020. "Institutions' Approach to Sexuality, A Necessity Between Care and Sexual Rights." *Soins. Psychiatrie,* 41 (330):12-16. https://doi.org/10.1016/s0241-6972(20)30100-6. PMID: 33353601.

---

1. https://www.scielo.br/j/estpsi/a/MLrZhVDnWCGknN6SBcn5kFq/?lang=pt

Goodman, Benny. 2013. "Erving Goffman and the Total Institution." *Nurse Education Today*, 33 (2): 81-81.

Goffman, Erving. 1961. *Asylums: Essays on the Social Situation of Mental Patients and Other Inmates*. New York: Anchor Books.

Henslin. James. 2014. "Chapter 3: Socialization." *Instructor's Manual, Essentials of Sociology*. London: Pearson.

Jenness, Valerie, and Gerlinger, Julie. 2020. "The Feminization of Transgender Women in Prisons for Men: How Prison as a Total Institution Shapes Gender." *Journal of Contemporary Criminal Justice* 36 (2): 1-24. https://doi.org/10.1177/1043986219894422

Madden, James John. 2010. Monastic Regime at Banyo Seminary: An Oral and Social History of the Pius XII Seminary, Banyo (1941-2000). PhD Thesis Doctor of Philosophy. University of Southern Queensland.

Oakley, Fr David. 2017. "Seminary Education and Formation: The Challenges and Some Ideas about Future Developments." *International Studies in Catholic Education*, 9 (2): 223-235, https://doi.org/10.1080/19422539.2017.1360613[2].

Optatam Totius [Decree on Priestly Training]. 1965. Decree on Priestly Training by Pope Paul VI on October 28, 1965. Vatican: Vatican Archives.

Malacrida, Claudia. 2005. "Discipline and dehumanization in a total institution: institutional survivors' descriptions of Time-Out Rooms." *Disability & Society*, 20(5), 523–537. doi:10.1080/09687590500156238.

Scott, Susie. 2010. "Revisiting the Total Institution: Performative Regulation in the Reinventive Institution." *Sociology* 44 (2): 213–231. Doi: 10.1177/0038038509357198.

---

2. https://doi.org/10.1080/19422539.2017.1360613

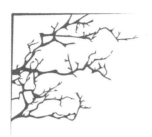

Chapter 4

My Early Seminary Years

Photo: Chapel at Night **Credit:** Free-Images.com

The Catholic seminary as what the sociologist Erving Goffman calls "total institution" follows a structured and regimented life. Like a military camp, the members follow certain rules and rigid daily schedule that is monitored by authorities. In a Catholic seminary, it is usually the duty of the Prefect of Discipline and the Rector to ensure that the daily schedule is always followed. At the end of every semester in my college seminary, the seminarian is evaluated not just in terms of academic performance, socialization, and spiritual life but also in terms of discipline and obedience to seminary rules. If he is

Seminary Schedule

GOD'S CALL: WHY I ENTERED THE SEMINARY

As a total institution, seminary life is structured and governed by a bell to inform seminarians for each activity. Every week, a seminarian is usually assigned as the bell ringer, and he rang the bell 5 minutes before the next activity. As far as I can remember, this was the daily schedule during weekdays.

Morning
5:00-5:30 Rise
5:30-6:00 Wash-Up
6:00-6:15 Morning Praise
6:15-7:00 Holy Mass
7:00-7:45 Breakfast
8:15-10:15 Classes
10:15-10:30 Snacks
10:30-11:30 Classes
11:45-12:00 Angelus
12:00-12:45 Lunch

Afternoon
1:00-2:00 Siesta (Afternoon Nap)
2:00-2:30 Rise/Wash-up
2:30-3:30 Classes
3:30-3:45 Snacks
3:45-4:45 "Manualia" (House Cleaning)
4:45-5:45 Sports
5:45-6:15 Wash-Up
6:15-7:00 Evening Praise/Personal Reflection
7:00-7:45 Dinner
7:45-9:30 Study Period
9:30-9:45 Night Prayer
9:45 Sleeping Time

On Sundays, seminarians attended Masses together with outsiders early in the morning. After lunch, we were allowed to visit our families or go to the city to buy personal items or even watch movies. But we should back before 6:00 o' clock in the evening for the Sunday benediction of the Blessed Sacrament. The evening was usually spent for indoor games, socialization, or study.

No Women: The Seminary as the Training Ground for Celibacy

Entering the seminary implies letting go of women in your life to live the celibate life. To encourage seminarians to live a chaste and celibate life, most professors, spiritual directors, and seminary personnel were male ordained priests. There were few women teaching during my time. I remember having one sister or nun as my professor in English literature. Another lay woman teaching biology and natural sciences. But philosophy and religion classes are taught by priests. We seminarians only had the opportunity to see young lay women during Sunday Masses where outsiders are allowed to join the celebration. We could also meet women during our short weekly break on Sunday afternoons.

Most seminarians who enter the college seminary are young heterosexual males who just graduated from high school. Some did not have sufficient experience dating with women in order to appreciate what they are giving up if they become celibate priests. Thus, it not difficult to see understand why seminarians would want more women as their teachers. I could really sense that seminarians gave special attention to their lay female teachers.

One time, our seminary Rector hired his beautiful newly graduate niece, Miss L., to teach biology for seminarians. Miss L. was a stunner being a former college muse! It seemed every seminarian was attracted to her inside the seminary! She was indeed very pretty. I was not sure that this was intentional on the part of our Rector to test our commitment to celibacy. However, the gazing eyes of seminary fathers and the celibacy rule had prevented seminarians to court her inside and outside the seminary premises. She just lived in a middle-class village near the seminary. In fact, some seminarians visited her during Sunday breaks.

The special attention given for Miss L. only indicated the strong psychological need of heterosexual seminarians for personal intimacy with the opposite sex. Her oozing femininity had indeed reenkindled the seminarians' need for psychosexual intimacy and romantic relationship, which could have been easily addressed if the priestly formation is apprenticeship where candidates lived their normal ordinary life in society while undergoing clerical education in a secular college or unity and spiritual formation under a veteran priest or bishop.

Miss L's beauty had awakened one seminarian's manic depression. He was formerly affiliated with a religious seminary before he joined our diocesan seminary. I learned that he was already diagnosed with some mental illness, but owing to the usual lack of professional psychologists and psychiatrists in most diocesan seminaries who can screen the applicant's psychosexual life, he was able to enter our seminary.

It is often the academic ability of the applicant that is strictly scrutinized by diocesan vocation directors and seminary formators. This guy is very intelligent, very friendly, and obedient to seminary rules, but he had a hidden psychological problem. In ordinary interaction, one can sense that he has repressed psychological problem, especially on women and social acceptance.

Photo: Depressed Man **Credit:** Free-Images.com

Miss L. has activated his "dormant" psychological issue. This guy became madly in love with her teacher Miss L. and often attempted to court her. One Sunday afternoon during weekly break, he found the right opportunity to visit and express her true romantic feelings to Miss L. According to the story circulated inside the seminary, this seminarian visited Miss L. in her home and revealed his strong love and affection for her. This guy is not good-looking, and Miss L. already had a boyfriend. She was probably annoyed by his courtship because her response to him was insulting: "If you and a dog are courting me, I would rather say "yes" to the dog and not to you!"

This seminarian immediately left her and returned to our seminary deeply depressed. Miss L's rejection has reactivated his psychological

GOD'S CALL: WHY I ENTERED THE SEMINARY 49

problem. The following morning, while we seminarians were praying the morning praise inside the chapel, we suddenly heard a loud shout, "Praise the Lord Alleluia!" Everyone was surprised and was asking whose voice was that. Some seminarians traced the voice in our dormitory and rushed to know who he was. In one of the shower rooms, they found this seminarian who was rejected by Miss L. kneeling and crying.

The seminary Rector and Prefect of Discipline immediately brought him to a psychiatrist in the city who confirmed that he was indeed suffering from a mental problem and his rejection from Ms. L. had reawakened it. The seminary eventually advised him to leave and return to his family. This whole story revealed the unintended problem of housing priestly candidates in a total institution, which is isolated from society. Separating priestly candidates from the real world can result in psychosexual immaturity, which cannot make seminarians mature individuals once ordained to the priesthood. In fact, most studies showed that mandatory celibacy and priestly training in an isolated, all-male, exclusive seminary training are major contributory factors for the persistence of clerical sexual misconduct.

Celibacy and Clergy Sexual Misconduct

Sands (2003, 79) argues that the "Church's sins against women and its abuse of children are founded in the priesthood's male-only character, its conceptualization as cultic and sacramental, its sexual asceticism, and its celibacy rule. The male-only character of the priesthood sets the foundation for the abuse of women by excluding women from power and idolizing the image of God as male."

Yip (2003, 60) also contends that the endurance of clergy sexual misconduct by celibate priests reflects the "culture of repression and secrecy" within the RCC, where open discussion about sexuality and relationship with women are generally prohibited. And Catholic seminaries as the primary institution for the formation of celibate priests in the RCC share this ineptitude and culture of repression and secrecy in dealing sexuality issues.

All male heterosexual Catholic priests accused and found guilty of CSA underwent the same human formation and gender role socialization in the celibate seminary formation set by the RCC for all candidates to Catholic priesthood. In the 11th and 12th centuries, the Second and Fourth Lateran Councils decreed the mandatory clerical celibacy for all Catholic clerics, resulting in the abandonment of the long tradition of the clerical training by apprenticeship and the adoption of celibate seminary training as the only method of clerical formation.

The apprenticeship clerical training allows the option of married priesthood and the continuation of normal socialization of clerical candidates in society while undergoing clerical training. But the secluded and all-male clerical seminary training, which is ideal for religious and monastic priests with the rare gift of celibacy, is separated from the real world.

. In clerical training for Catholic priests, the RCC expects seminary formators to spiritually form seminarians according to its official teachings on celibate priesthood and the perfect celibate masculinity (Keenan 2015). Although Christ originally taught optional celibacy and married priesthood has been existing in the Western Church in some form since the time of the apostles up to the present, the RCC imposed clerical celibacy in the 11th and 12th centuries that only allowed celibate priesthood as ideal model for Catholic priesthood (Ballano 2023).

This adoption of celibate priesthood as the only recognized universal calling for Catholic priesthood has shifted the gender socialization for priestly candidates in Catholic seminaries in favor of candidates who are able to live chaste and celibate heterosexual life like Christ.

Premonition of the Call for Become an Author

I really don't have an idea that my calling is not really to become a priest but a Catholic sociologist and author. Recalling the past, I think there was already a great urge within me to do greater things for the Catholic Church. I was thinking of writing books with creative titles such as "Forging Ahead" or the "Future of the Catholic Church", etc.

It just dawned into my mind how the Catholic Church should face the ever-changing contemporary society to pursue its spiritual mission. This seemed prophetic. Currently, I am started to write these ideas in a new book I am currently writing on how the Catholic Church should look like in the third millennium using the sociological-theological approach.

When I entered the seminary, there was no existing school organ or newsletter that allowed seminarians to publish their spiritual and philosophical reflections. In college Catholic seminaries, seminaries usually take philosophy as the major course. Thus, seminarians are trained to use philosophical reasoning to analyze social issues. The examinations in our philosophy subjects were all in essays. And I was thinking that some of these essays should be published in a school organ for other to read.

I really did not have a passion for writing when I was in high school. Art and painting—yes! Since I am also an artist. I joined some school art competitions and won. From first year to fourth year high school, I was also preoccupied with sports not writing, playing soccer in division and regional competition together with some of my classmates, although we maintain our grades as students of the top section. I became a soccer athlete for the regional Northern Mindanao Athletic Association (NMAA), which competes with other cities and provinces within the region. I became part of the province's junior soccer team together with some of my classmates.

Becoming a writer was far from my mind when I was in high school. That is why after 40 years when I was named one of the top alumni for the year 2022 in the field of sociology, my classmates were surprised that I became the most academic of my class and batch and not my salutatorian and valedictorian classmates. God indeed has plans for everyone.

References

Ballano, Vivencio O. 2023. *In Defense of Married Priesthood: A Sociotheological Investigation of Catholic Clerical Celibacy*. London: Routledge.

Brown, Peter. 2008. The Body and Society: Men, Women, and Sexual Renunciation in Early Christianity, Twentieth Anniversary Edition with a New Introduction. New York, NY: Columbia University Press.

Daly, Brendan. 2009. "Priestly Celibacy: The Obligations of Continence and Celibacy for Priests." Compass: A Review of Topical Theology 43 (4): 20-33. http://compassreview.org/pdf/summer09.pdf.

Daniel, Kasomo. 2012. "The Psychology Behind Celibacy." International Journal of Psychology and Behavioral Sciences 2 (4): 88-93. https://doi.org/10.5923/j.ijpbs.20120204.03.

Issaco, Anthony, Ethan Sahker, and Elizabeth Krinock. 2015. "How Religious Beliefs and Practices Influence the Psychological Health of Catholic Priests." American Journal of Men's Health 10 (4): 325-337. https://doi.org/10.1177/1557988314567325.

Keenan, Marie. 2015. "Masculinity, Relationships and Context: Child Sexual Abuse and the Catholic Church Catholic Church." *Irish Journal of Applied Social Studies* 15 (2): 64-77.

Lea, Henry Charles. 2003. The History of Sacerdotal Celibacy in the Christian Church. Honolulu, Hawaii: University Press of the Pacific.

Mayblin, Maya. 2018. "A Brilliant Jewel: Sex, Celibacy, and the Roman Catholic Church." Religion 49 (4): 517-538. https://doi.org/10.1080/0048721X.2018.1525774.

Owen, Helen L. 2001. When Did the Catholic Church Decide Priests Should Be Celibate? History News Network. Oct 2001. https://historynewsnetwork.org/article/696.

Sands, Kathleen M. 2003. "Speaking Out: Clergy Sexual Abuse: Where Are the Women?" *Journal of Feminist Studies in Religion* 19 (2): 79–83. http://www.jstor.org/stable/25002477.

Sipe, A. W. Richard. 1990. A Secret World: Celibacy and the Search for Celibacy. New York: Brunner/Mazel.

Yip, Andrew. K. T. 2003. "Sexuality and the Church." *Sexualities* 6(1): 60–64. https://doi.org/10.1177/1363460703006001007.

---

[1] Biblegateway. n.d. "Scripture Engagement." https://www.biblegateway.com/resources/scripture-engagement/contemplate/home.

Don't miss out!

Visit the website below and you can sign up to receive emails whenever Vivencio Ballano publishes a new book. There's no charge and no obligation.

https://books2read.com/r/B-A-ELMKC-EELAF

BOOKS 2 READ

Connecting independent readers to independent writers.

Did you love *God's Call: Why I Entered the Seminary*? Then you should read *"We are God's Children Too!": Resisting Homophobia and Natural Law for Full LGBTQI Integration in the Catholic Church*[1] by Vivencio Ballano!

[2]

This book affirms the human dignity of the members of the LGBTQI as Children of God who should be fully accepted in the Catholic Church. It sociologically analyzes how institutional homophobia or fear of homosexuality and the traditional natural law morality that only allows heterosexuality and gender complementarity of male and female constitute the primary ecclesial and conceptual hindrance toward the full integration of the gender-diverse LGBTQI in the Catholic Church. It recommends the updating of the Church's natural moral framework and adoption of a sociological-synodal moral framework to overcome

---

1. https://books2read.com/u/booWLp

2. https://books2read.com/u/booWLp

homophobia and unconditionally welcome the gay community in the Catholic Church with full moral rights like heterosexuals as God's Children.

Read more at https://www.researchgate.net/profile/Vivencio-Ballano/stats.

Also by Vivencio Ballano

Gender and the Catholic Church
Why Can't Pope Francis and the Catholic Church Fully Accept the LGBTQI?: A Sociological-Synodal Exploration and Solution
"We are God's Children Too!": Resisting Homophobia and Natural Law for Full LGBTQI Integration in the Catholic Church
"We're Not an Ideology But Persons With Human Dignity"

My Religious Vocation and Journey Vol. 1
God's Call: Why I Entered the Seminary

Watch for more at https://www.researchgate.net/profile/Vivencio-Ballano/stats.

About the Author

Dr. Vivencio "Ven" Ballano holds a master's degree in Catholic theology and a doctorate in sociology from the Jesuit-run Ateneo de Manila University, Manila, Philippines. He is currently the Program Chairperson of the master's degree program in sociology at the Polytechnic University of the Philippines (PUP). To date, Dr. Ballano has published 7 Scopus-indexed books and 3 more forthcoming ones in 2024 and 2025 with imprints Springer Nature and Routledge.

Read more at https://www.researchgate.net/profile/Vivencio-Ballano/stats.

Milton Keynes UK
Ingram Content Group UK Ltd.
UKHW040715141024
449705UK00001B/84